BOAT BURNED

KELLY GRACE THOMAS

Boat Burned

 YESYES BOOKS *Portland*

BOAT BURNED © 2020 BY KELLY GRACE THOMAS

FIRST EDITION

COVER ART © "THE NOONE" © LARA ZANKOUL, 2014

COVER & INTERIOR DESIGN: ALBAN FISCHER

ISBN 978-1-936919-72-7

PRINTED IN THE UNITED STATES OF AMERICA

LIBRARY OF CONGRESS CATALOGING-IN-PUBLICATION

DATA IS AVAILABLE UPON REQUEST.

PUBLISHED BY YESYES BOOKS

1614 NE ALBERTA ST

PORTLAND, OR 97211

YESYESBOOKS.COM

KMA SULLIVAN, PUBLISHER

STEVIE EDWARDS, SENIOR EDITOR, BOOK DEVELOPMENT

ALBAN FISCHER, GRAPHIC DESIGNER

DEVI GONZALES, MANAGING EDITOR

COLE HILDEBRAND, SENIOR EDITOR OF OPERATIONS

LUTHER HUGHES, ASSISTANT EDITOR & YYB TWITTER

AMBER RAMBHAROSE, EDITOR, ART LIFE & INSTAGRAM

CARLY SCHWEPPE, ASSISTANT EDITOR, *VINYL*

ALEXIS SMITHERS, ASSISTANT EDITOR, *VINYL* & YYB FACEBOOK

PHILLIP B. WILLIAMS, COEDITOR IN CHIEF, *VINYL*

AMIE ZIMMERMAN, EVENTS COORDINATOR

HARI ZIYAD, ASSISTANT EDITOR, *VINYL*

For my family, Omid, and the ocean

"When your army has crossed the border, you should burn your boats…"
—SUN TZU

After the trip has ended, one still feels the ocean rocking beneath one's feet. The whole room sways as if the house were floating atop an ocean. You get seasick while sleeping in the suburbs. You never stop hearing the ship's bell, quietly but symphonically ringing the hours of your watch.

There is no cure. Sometimes the only remedy is to get back on a boat, to go back to sea.

Which is to say, some part of me remains tied to Her mast.
— ROBIN COSTE LEWIS

CONTENTS

VESSELED

Here's how it happened:
I burned each boat
but first they flamed
me. I knew what I was:
a vessel he could float

inside. He boarded me.
I burned. He hammered
my hips. Violence: a type of marriage.
Maybe I wanted to be owned.

I won't tell you
about the anchor.
How it rusts
like a fist. He became
my gravity. If I am not boat
then what?

In another life, I stood
treetall. Growled at every axe.
It started when Noah
made an ark of me.

It started when a storm
knuckled my roots right out.
Yes, I stood too close.
Now I am made
from his wood. Lacquered,
conditioned to heel.
To throw my body
lopside at wind. A salty
bride. A keel inside
my stomach.

Don't you know how near drowning
sits? This isn't something I can throw
overboard. I won't go back.

I build my fire in boats.
I build my boats with fire.

Go ahead, call me a blaze
behind my back.

The ocean, my witness,
watches the body cross
itself. I hold a match
to everything I no longer am.

I

The cure for anything is salt water: sweat, tears, or the sea.

—ISAK DINESEN

MAL DE DÉBARQUEMENT

Diagnosis: Land sick.
Experience stutters
in the pores. Thirsts
for boat. Muscles moan
ocean. The body's small stories
bow to another gravity. Salt
fiend. You mourn
for your mother. The movement
of her earth. Rise and fall.
The rock. She swelled you
to sleep. Sung a sea inside
these bones. Symptoms: Balance
fools across generations.
Convinces the body it is owned
enough to get a name. The dirt sways.
Skyscrapers bob like seagulls. Nothing solid
holds. You rock. Chartless
with nowhere stars. Small
relief in anything man
made. Cars. Trains. But when you still
the memory muddies. Seasick with the ways
you were taught to woman.

To altar absent men.

You break. Over and over, like waves.

Causes: You once told your mother

you could be anything. *Yes*, she said. *Even a wife.*

Let him confuse you for freedom. Confuse body

for boat. You rise and fall.

The rhythm of what you've been

taught. Cells hoard. Three fourths

of her. Hunger blankets this earth.

Once a mother gives birth

she never stops speaking.

Treatment: Almost all cases:

female. No tie between the length

of the trip, how bad the symptoms or how long

they will last. The body sways trying

to out rock a bigger body. Name its own ground.

Cure: There is none. You can go back. Give

in. Return to boat. Or keep on, unsteady, never trust

what promises to keep, to stay. But if symptoms

do not remit. Depart on their own

terms. The disorder remains.

Incurable, permanent.

HOW THE BODY IS PASSED DOWN

My mother unzips the body.
Passes it down.

The dress tailored
too tight. Leaves red

indentation of buttons.
Pressed hard as apology.

My mother was still hungry. Royal
with fridge glow. Learned

that loneliness
eats with its hands.

My body has always been
a window I cannot throw myself

from. Breasts stomach thighs
dimpled and swollen. Wetted

wood in a house I was born
into. But did not build.

I see my mother's hips
every time I open

the fridge. Every time
the fridge opens me.

My cabinets stocked
with shame. What a mother

feeds her young.
Now I know

a body can haunt
itself. Be a fear

no one else believes in.
A ghost

that only says
my name.

HALF-MASTED

The flag speaks his victims
but doesn't name them.
Doesn't look them in the eye.

We walk, it's almost breakfast
early Ohio sunrise. Everything
around us open, growing.

And then we see it.

My friend tells me she can't remember
a time when the flags were not
half-mast.
This is not how
days are supposed to start.

So I ask
about the most recent tragedy.
And she says *pick one*.
We shrug.

And now cities are blown-out candles
lit for vigil. And now flags hang
head down
limp from poles.

A discarded dress, messy on my bedroom floor.
A dress I used to love.

It lays there, dismissed.
Folded into itself.

A surrender of whichever way it met
the ground.

I can't bring myself to throw it out.

I'm not sure I want to wear
America anymore.

What to do with things that used to make us
feel beautiful?

THE BOAT OF MY BODY

He tugged at my skirt. Said: *vessel*.
He hoisted me down. Yelled: *voyage*.

Yes, I am boat. Was born
half forest. Still think about that axe.

I want to smell like mahogany
again. I want all these hands

out of my cabin.

Not to mention the oars,
forced down the mouths
of rivers.

Noah was the first.

He said: *Here is everything
left of this world.*

Carry it for me. Your belly speaks.

A soft, wet float.

ANCHORED TO SOMETHING DEEP

My father introduced me to ocean.
What it meant to divorce
the earth. I moored myself

to distance. Studied leaving
like a chart. Family, another word
for horizon. The wait turned me:

a dark buoy. An empty bell
soaked in deeper water. I rock
for his return. Anchored

to everything absent. Coast-
lines crash. The riptide of reflection.
I can't see—night on night.

Romance written in our wake.

The weight of a necklaced name.

Its hands around my throat.

I SUGGEST OMID SHAVE HIS BEARD

And I hate myself for it.
But it could be the difference
between whether he comes home
or not.

Half this country
sees beard and thinks
bomb. Thinks Muslim
means murder.
And that half
looks just like me.

Omid's beard grows
fast with my worry. I fear
that half will never consider
the softness of his smile.
That Persians are poets.
That the sun rises
in the East.

At night, I run
my fingers through his

beard. The razor
of the nightly news
pressed. And I'm not sure

I can't keep
either of us safe.

The day after the election
he tells me: *terror*
is being caught in the crosshairs
of a white man's gaze.
Half this country has eyes
like a loaded gun.

After I ask, he turns
to me and says *Yes*
I am scared.
But I will never shave
myself away
so more of this
can grow.

STORM WARNING

She told me: *pain*
needs a witness.

Knowing, once
or twice, the fruit of me
has been peeled.

Under this dress: eggs
and arms. A one-eyed

doll:
       births
             and
                  breaks.

I live under shell-cracked
sky. Sleep with unbalanced

bones. Female: a storm
I first noticed
in the clouds.

It has taken all

      of me

          to rain

              this hard.

WE KNOW MONSTERS BY THEIR TEETH

But what of a woman
without canines. One who has lost
the muscle of molars. Prisoner to a bite
that only knows: *run.*

Inside this mouth I was once wolf.

Now only a dress of pink
shriveled gums that whisper:

Excuse me. Not here.
I'm not even here.

The small death of letting
go. Rest a four-letter word.
My bed a shallow grave. Every morning
I'm a shovel of knees, every night
an earthworm of goodbye.
Lifting from soil.

This is the dirt
of never coming home.

                                               I can remember
                                when the first tooth fell.

The first time I monstered
or womaned

                                 and someone was there
                                            to watch.

Maybe I'm whatever evil you want
to name me. Maybe I'm not
the tooth.
But the empty space

                                 I tongue into small coffins

when there is no more
strength
to chew.

CLOSER

My father left us

like weather. My mother sunk

next to the dock. Us daughters tried

to swim, became driftwood in the back-

yard. I am still somewhere.

Stuck at ten. Trying

to call a shipwreck home.

The past scolds *look at her*

blueburnt and barnacled.

I wash my mouth out

with waves. *Closer*, it says.

Her fiberglass dress.

She itches. Memory blooms:

a rash. I scratch

to bleed. History is a dirty

ocean. And I am dangerous

with thirst. Most days, I schooner.

Wait, nets empty. I can't wind

the strength. Most nights, I drink

story or language. I can't keep

either down.

WHERE NO ONE SAYS EATING DISORDER

When I was young, I pretended
we weren't sick. Three women.
Three rooms. The body
a dark teacher. My sister studied
evacuation. Tried to expel
it all. Greedy with knowledge
she wouldn't let the stomach
out-fact her. My mother hoarded
everything inside. Bunkered her body
so no one could leave it
again. I took almost nothing.
My mother changed
the subject when I cried
at each bite. Found a backpack full
of diet pills. Told me I had wasted
my money trying to disappear.

She didn't know how to heal
the quiet between us. Starved
for food. (Men.)
Attention its own
meal. The small gods

we let control us.
We were so hungry
for anything
to love us back.

OMID TELLS ME YOU'VE BEEN LOOKING LESS PUFFY LATELY

I do not thank him / Instead think about undressing / All those exhausted nights
      before bed / his eyes / tracking each curve / sifting through words

I relive each moment / he has seen me / naked / Doughy / a kneaded / rising loaf / I break
      bread / backward / I spill /portions and measures

Mother's recipe / poured down / from shaky liver / spotted hands / and before her
      Mother's mother / Tonight I call / grandma's

blue birds / to sing / me still / Paint me back / to Botticelli / where I rise
      fully formed from sea / Buoyed / by my own / round reach / A bellyful

feast / to forgive each famine / the curation of concave / I want to meet a mouth hungrier
      than mine / A yield of yeast / that doesn't wish / to flatten / I know / he meant it

to be kind / As if to say / *honey* / *restraint* / *wears you well* / But under my clothes
      I still feel / fingerprints / of flour / I want to tell him / but then he will

look / Instead / I turn / out the lights / undress in dark / and beg / to be unmade

IN AN ATTEMPT TO SOLVE FOR X: FEMININITY AS WORD PROBLEM

Possible answers: Don't say
the word *body*. Or become
a slow crawl of thigh highs.
Divide every possible solution
by *Remember this was your idea*.

True or False: When solving
for *y* the answer to diet pills
is more diet pills. Genetics
is a mean hammer. The difference
between shame and guilt is showing
your work.

Word problem as map: You
are the smallest place you know.
Possible steps to solving for y (you)
1) Give back the rib 2) Eat every apple
until you are fat with orchards 3) Dress
in snake and dig a grave.

Word problem. Version Two. Russian nesting
doll daughter (into) wife (into) mother.
Find the lowest common denominator. Divide
the fractions among many mouths. Ideal
answers: Tell the junior at UCLA
you have the answer. Use words like *better now*
then walk her to her car. Do not tell her
like you, she will always be hungry.

Possible problem: Your mother laughed
when you disappeared. Possible answer: You
are still suspect. So is she. Acceptable
answer: You have not finished disappearing.
Plus, you are still thirsty for bones.

II

The man who has experienced shipwreck shudders even at a calm sea.

—OVID

PORTRAIT OF A ROOFLESS HOUSE

I wish we could talk
about   lonely.
I come from a house
made of women.
Taught that men
would be their shelter.
Men that thought a roof
was enough. Thirst loosened
the tar. Peeled off each
shingle like a wedding band.
We live in downpour.
Still no one mentions
being wet. The centuries
without power.
Instead we overhang
the memory of men
who somewhere-elsed.
I raised myself
to expect men
to leave.
The Dear John
of geography. Sticks

and stones still rotting
in my hands.
The story rained
so hard, it's all I had
to drink. Hope is the loneliest
house on the block.
It spends years waiting
for a hammer. Forgets
it was once a tree.

JUMPING BEANS: AMTRAK 1991

I clutch a fistful of jumping beans.
Grip frozen, knuckled. This last thing
I will not lose.

They're a parting gift, father said.
Something to remind you
to smile.

On the train ride back
to Jersey, the beans jump
in my sweaty hands.
We both fight
for breath
inside our tiny
glass box. I palm
them like a parent.

I whisper to the beans,
Promise. Promise you won't leave.
My mother museum-silent
stares at the slipping Carolina
coast.

I haven't stopped crying since Florida.
The other passengers worry.
There are five more states to go.

My mother shakes her head.
Tucks sunbleached hair behind
my ear. Pulls me close. Kisses
each cry quiet. Whispers, *honey*
the tighter you hold on
the more they will want
to run.

After exhaustion takes
what it's owed
I awake. Hands cold. Empty.

The beans have found another home.

DAD LET US NAME THE BOAT: *ROMANCE*

We could have chosen any word
Still young enough to have faith

My sister and I thought: repeat
something enough it might

eventually appear Now
I know I will never be

beautiful enough
Too many

pretty ports
to keep men

still As a girl I thought *desire*
could float

us all Sundays my family
sailed An almost shipwreck

I prayed
for wind

After the divorce
Days no longer

our(s) desire could
not float

Pretty ports shipwreck
a girl Sail a family

to almost father
days to name

Romance If I repeat
myself enough

I might eventually
appear

I no longer
sail on Sundays

There is never
any wind

DARK BUOY

The ocean is twice as deep
at night. A family
14 miles out.
Off the Jacksonville coast.
A syllable
in the sea's mouth.
My father saw
it first. Inches from us.
The buoy. 30 feet
high. Bulb burnt
out. Ready to bite.
Chomp our hull
in half. Dad spun
the wheel. The boat
lurched. We spilled
bodies. Reached for something
stable. No one knew
where we were. Not even us.
The dark buoy deserted. Ships miles
from touch. The clutch of loneliness
can bend bones. Yes, we survived.
But I can still smell its rust. I imagine

the if of impact. Our boat: splintered,
swollen, sunk. The bell of neglect
still ringing to no one. Ignored.
Tethered to the same spot.
How it is dangerous
to leave
something chained up
so long.

HOW MY MOTHER (ALMOST) DIED

Maybe it started with the cracking of ribs, the breaking of birdhouses made from popsicle sticks. There was anesthesia and surgical masks. There was a man in a white coat trying to bring her back. There were daughters from California, who sat next to her hospital bed. Patient ferns, hoping to share their oxygen.

Maybe it was the Christmas her eyes became frightened owls in a foreign forest. Her hands shaky as wind chimes. She always loved the holidays, always decorated the house before our visit. She whispered *something's very wrong*, holding the undercooked turkey.

Maybe it was when her handwriting changed. On the Valentine's card she sent me, I spotted the tremor in her g's, the fracture of her s's. She became a shattered alphabet.

Maybe it was when she looked in the mirror and only saw her own mother's paper skin.

Maybe it was at her father's funeral. Her lips a padlock she placed in the coffin. A dying secret she palmed into a stiff, granite hands. A violin chord before black veils and loose dirt.

Maybe it started at her child's fifth birthday, with that third piece of cake. Sugared roses never wilt. The way taste can lurk as understudy, practicing its lines for lonely lips.

Maybe it was when her husband left. When he said, *it's over, no more*. His two daughters, silent at the dinner table. Leaving the knife still dirty on the plate.

REASONS I HAVEN'T DONE THE DISHES

Because what can compete with a dying mother.

Because that tide has been rising.

Because there are so many ways to be a glass of water.

Because people don't know how to say *I know this is hard*

when *this is hard* is hard to say.

Because no matter what mood I wore to dinner,

I need you to still be here.

Because I feel sorry for myself in bubble baths.

Because I've spent my life barking.

Because there are still wounds to lick no one can hear.

Because I wonder how you miss me.

Because I live in Los Angeles where the coyotes get hit by cars.

Because the mountains are moving closer.

Because this soft, wet animal is something I'm not.

Because I am ugly and frightened at the watering hole.

Because I don't like asking to be fed.

MY FATHER TELLS ME PELICANS BLIND THEMSELVES

searching for food.
       Diving head first. Eyes
              open: suicide.

They starve into myth.
       And hatch hungry
              children. They peck

at parents who strike
       back. The young revived
              by drip of father's blood.

Or booze. Today there are leaks
       I cannot hold.
              I have spilled too much.

Appetite: my deepest
       grave. This family
              flies to silent

corners. Until we bleed
and bird again.
I've drunk

all the body
this wine will allow.
Boatburned, I kneel.

Father, rock me
like a child.
Sing me to sea.

DAUGHTER

Jotted gospel/transparent as sky/light/Basement or bassinet/Wedding china/Pinch of prayers between shoulders/Every ocean/empty/into drain/Downstream/a tuna laced in mercury/Hook and bait/Part stomach/part swallow/A hymn/a history/a hurt/The song singing an empty room to sleep/Knows the second story/father built/another house another woman/Remembers the dinner/table grew/Fingers that run/all this touch/over hysteria/of bones/All this birth/blame/bloat/Borrowed and blue/Be told *stay home*/Be told *pretty burn/too bright/they call it arso*n

THE POLITE BIRD OF STORY

Takes flight, against God or the sky.
We are always open domes looking for rest.

The linoleum stung with spill.
The cabinets full of hard parts.

I have been thinking about the shells
of Russian Dolls snapping like twigs

under the hunter's footsteps.
The way each woman looks in the mirror and

sees the window a sparrow flew into.
Sometimes there is too much female—

they call it monster. I roil a tiny teakettle
behind these picket teeth. Perfection

a cold cup of tea. This menu of vacancy, I chew
and chew. Please don't watch me eat.

The living room for sitting. The bedroom for silence.
Mother waits like winter. Father speaks in drywall.

I daughter into still life. Spend hours drying
a roped-off smile.

In this world there are kitchens and there
are mothers. Both cold like the sky left waiting.

Food is just another ghost story
the starved like to tell.

MY THERAPIST ASKS HOW THE DOLLHOUSE WAS BUILT

My hands rest
on my stomach.
The retaining wall: emaciated.
I try not to remember
the missing front door.
Every kitchen: upside down.
The blades of the blender:
a bloody crown.
Hunger: a throne
I have always feared.

And your father? she asks.
Always with a hammer,
I say. His voice: a level.
He was there, as much as distance
allowed. My mother: frozen in the 50s
spoiling in the kitchen. She hoarded
tradition. At the dinner table I ate
myself empty. Scraped the want
from china. I thirst for shelter
I have no faith in. My body: a church
where no one prays.

THE HOUSES I'VE BUILT

We must build houses for our mothers in our poems

—ARACELIS GIRMAY

After school I did what any girl might: cursed
Algebra, snuck in a smoke, thought
about the bodies that raised
us. The blackouts and
parties. I gave myself
away for an ugly swig
of eyes. Mom, I can't blame you
for these walls. The weight
of the word wife.
Always so heavy.
But I want to be more
than what I please. I am learning
to say no. To build my own
roof. But I call you crying and you ask
about Omid first. Worry
he has left me. Worry each meal
will have an empty seat that looks
like him. You gave too much.
Gave your life away

to man or memory.
Mom, I built this book
for you. Tell me a kitchen table
secret. Let's heirloom each other.
Turn shame to sanctuary. This is more
like love. Please know I have always
named you saint. You are beautiful
with or without him. But let me speak
this sadness. Build these poems.
I will keep saying *no*. There will still be joy.
We bloom a January flower. Every daughter
is owed these words. Even you. Especially you.

REPLAY

It started with silence
a coastline ate through me. Salt or song
spilled me into this sail.
I try to write an honest goodbye
stanzas splintered like oar or father.
For thirty days we sailed together, apart.

Shoved inside, I swallowed storm. A part
of me never knew water. Just a body. Silence
craves any word for God besides—Father
the deeper I drink the heavier the song.
Now the ocean only means goodbye
a patchwork of stanzas and troubled sails.

I warn myself don't write (about family). I whisper *sail
away*. Let childhood drift apart.
But a sailboat is the slowest goodbye,
a leaked lonely. The four of us in our cities of silence.
I've scribbled small mutinies. My words (weight, water) bloated. A song,
I release the anchor lines of mother, daughter, sister, father.

The ocean must miss someone too. Father
did you know this sail
boat would turn throat, a rusted ready song?
These dirges I can still smell in the dark, a part
of home that won't stop sinking. And this silence:
how many times will I frame this goodbye?

Please believe me. I only wanted to be good. By
now I have sacrificed the many names for father.
Or family. I gulped these ships of silence.
I was raised like a sail.
pulled like a sheet, fraying apart.
Our history reeking with song.

Mother swears this is not a sad song.
These things happen. My pages or years too long a goodbye.
My hands are itchy too. Ache a part
of every landscape I pen. Lonely the only wound I can father.
Every line I write luffs like a sail.
They ask *what happened*, I sink with silence.

I song the sometimes. Every time a man walks out I call him father.
Goodbye, a hungry seagull that won't stop cawing my name. The sail
like the story, is filthy with holes. Silence, another kind of wind.

III

Every woman begins as weather.

—PATRICIA SMITH

THE SURGEON GENERAL NAMES LONELINESS
A MEDICAL EPIDEMIC

I have seen what was named / woman revolt / I stomach vacancy / Ask science to put

its hands inside me / Bills that spread / like legs / Blame me / in apples / in children

I do not have / until I am only bite / Mouthful of rotten / *I'm sorrys* / naked / I interrogate

my organs / Gavel carved from thinning bone / I am a piece / of every ship / I've built and

sank / I lie / in a tub of language / Hope to wake up / clean

ARSON IS A FAMILY NAME

I soak in the bathtub
scrub the nightly news
from my skin.
The headlines
loud like the hands
of men. I soap
away the bluebird
song dying
in a bruised boy's chest.
I shampoo my hair
and empty classrooms
fall to the drain.
I scrub until I bleed
in protest.
But there is still America
underneath my nails.

ANOTHER FIGHT ABOUT OMID'S BEARD

My friends say *you should consider your surroundings*.
And all I hear is *you're surrounded*.

AFTER

The Bomb dropped.

Or the man got elected.

Or the girls were raped

and accused

of flirting. The testimonies

smeared like newsprint in the rain.

After it all they turned off

the cameras. Wiped away

each face. The ocean

has dried up.

Still we sink.

It's hard for a body

to prove anything

once it's been erased.

TO THE LOBSTER WE COOKED AT KENYON

In Ohio
I taught another writer

how to
kill.

How to divide
your tail

like a country.
Split open.

The butt of the knife
a new baton.

Your insides hardened
and I don't blame them.

He said: *slaughter.*
I said: *dinner.*

It didn't change
a thing. And what

remained? A leftover
hollowed shell

we covered
with a lid.

I TRY ON MY FIRST ONE PIECE IN THE DRESSING ROOM AT ROSS

Mouth open I stare
at what fluorescence makes
of my ass. I count
the dimples of cellulite.
My back fat folds
like a lowered flag
I've been meaning
to burn.

Every fourth of July we stay
with Omid's family
in Tahoe. They do not eat
bread. Their Persian bodies
thin as branches. We celebrate
a country no one wants
to love. The first time
his father saw my photo
he called me *chubby*.
Suggested his son
reconsider.

In Tahoe all the white women
        wear white. Their bodies
slender as the quaking aspens
        they sunbathe under.
My trunk is thick.
        I don't look
expensive. At the pool
        I take off my clothes.
I wait to bloom
        bride, to woman

the right way. In bed sheets
        soft as my stomach
Omid's hands beg:
        stay. But I am still
in the dressing room
        at Ross. Alone.
Staring at a body. After

        the barbeque
and fireworks
        I wake in the night.
I open the fridge and stare.
        His father keeps it
empty. Like the dressing room.

Like my stomach.
The stare of fluorescent washes
over me. I apologize
for all the places I find myself
hungry.

I AM NO WHITE DRESS

In the dimly lit diner, a man sips his coffee
says: *pass the hospital*.
On the table, funerals sit dirty on plates.
I look into his empty playground
and only hear grass stains.
There are no children, just ants.
Crawling, dying.

My hand shakes as I hold the hospital
across the table. Sickness spills into his coffee
like milk. Outbreak. A cold case of kitchens
and one night nevers. He raises his cup
and says: *to slaughter*.

We swim in vinegar until our smiles
are pickled as the sun. But this isn't our summer
never will be. I can't baseball or Babe Ruth.
I am no white dress. Only a spill of cavities
from the hospitals that wait in my mouth.

The waitress comes over to take our hunger
and asks: *over easy or scrambled?*
Over our heads the days float
away. Is this how we end

seasons? In the quiet corners of new
school clothes (that prove you change).
I place my hands next to my empty mug
and half-eaten cages.

I stare at the hospitals stuck
to the bottom of my cup.
I look at him, across the table
and say: *the sweeter we try*
to make it, the more disease
it will bring.

DRESSING

I know every way
I shouldn't be woman
Hands bloodied
from smile

A ritual: count the parts
of me
still talking
I don't write
about the wine
Instead broken stems
dying flowers
eggshelled walls
thinned to fist

Today I felt like choking
anything I could
wrap my hands around

Instead I bought a dress
to make a man
love me

Now one does

It doesn't fit

I WANT TO BE UNCLOTHED

as weather. To look into the mouths of hurricanes. Say *undress me like a building.*
Rain your lonely hammers. You and I are nothing but windows after they have been
shook. An empty glass, a hemisphere raising its tiny fists. My confessions float
face down. Eyes eaten out by fish. I am sinking things again. I always blame the
sky. Each thirst: a continent moving further and further from truth. The parts
of us that stumble. A two-footed loss or forecast. The ocean will never fit inside
this mouth. Tonight tides drip from my teeth. They told me this would happen.
The boats all dress in black.

HUNGER IS A BRIDE

A grave that doesn't fill.

Wing starved, she can only throat.

Birdseed in someone else's bed.

A body bouqueted

and budgeted. Waiting to be

named. Hunger hangs

like a dark chandelier. She's sick

with glass. Hunger takes a woman

like a vow. A list of small violences:

to have and to hold. An anniversary

of knives. I slaughtered

the tallest tree just to find this ring.

Hunger sits at the edge

of my bed. I am a small

surrender.

OWNED

Worry ruined the only black stilettos I own. Worry knows I hate my legs. How I'm flatfooted and ordinary. Thinks I look better in boots. Worry claws at the red freshly painted door, tore up the Crate and Barrel. Worry doesn't care: about cortisol, about twelvehour desklunches, about the boss that hired me to argue. Worry barks until it's fed. Worry worries I don't give enough. That even sleep is lazy. That I will be fat never full. Worry hungers. Begs for half my meal. Drools at the smell of blood: steak, bacon, thighs. Worry whimpers. Needs to be walked. Wants the neighborhood to see. Worry pisses on every flower. Knows some name it allergy. I told Worry I bought a cage. Worry barked so loud the neighbors heard. Worry hasn't had its shots. Worry: never neutered. Wants to breed. Wants to get on everything. Always says *look how fast I family. Look how many rooms I live in now.*

THE DOCTOR SAYS THE IUD IS LOST INSIDE ME

There are tiny metal arms
that refuse to ungrab
A greedy child burrows in my uterus
wants to be kept
But it's me who begs

This is what I get for wanting
everything but, for too many
years This body:

a board in a fence
that waits for men
to kick it in

Most days
I sicken of the boundaries
I do not draw

between them and myself
between myself and myself

Empty
as an evacuated prayer

LOST AT SEA

I circle the page hungry
as a boat

that can't remember
land. My hollow

hull more female
than float.

I was told
He named me

boat. My body written
by greedy hands.

But maybe
I did it

to myself.
I greet this sea

with slow sadness
a sail I raise

without wind.
That wine glass

is another type of ship.
The gust of grapes.

Drunk.
I have done it

all wrong.

I'LL NEVER RETURN

Omid tells me
I hold my breath.

But when I exhale
home falls

from my mouth. The floor-
boards spill from my lungs.

My skin a map of looking
back. I swallow every place

I cannot keep. Always
fear I'll never return.

The reason they call
division long.

My breath tightens with footsteps.
Even now I can't

remember the house of him.
God or father. Still I beg

for shelter. Don't mistake
persistence for roots.

My father was
a carpenter too.

I am
nowhere

close
to found.

WHAT THE NEIGHBORS SAW

Another dying doe: no.

A fist: sometimes.

Every tooth in the china cabinet: yes.

Open on a kitchen like handcuffs: yes.

Fridge full of food: yes.   All you hear

                                                        is   knives.

True.

Avocado: no.   A stick of softened butter: yes.

The mother: maybe.

        The instinct: never.

                The crime scene: every time.

Thumb pressed to butter: yes.

Like flowers dying: no.

Like the drains and the diapers: no.

                                        This is how we fingerprint.

The infant's sock. Pause. Blood, unwashed. Pause.
Keep the bedroom door closed: yes. But, no.
But have to: yes.
Don't think of blue daisies: no.
I don't.

The door a closed mouth: okay.
The therapist: *Do you blame yourself?* Sometimes: yes.

                                   I can't drive   tonight.

Do not say: *headlights*.
Never ask: *deer?*
And please god: don't talk about her age.

A lonely dinner table: no.
The   only   thing

to eat: yes.
The *how was your day*: sometimes.
The steering wheel breakdowns: often.

Breakdown and break in: just stage directions: yes.

And we can talk about tiny coffins: don't.
We can talk of eulogies.

The outloud of: this
                              No. Not yet, maybe.
I should.
No.

The fork scraping
        on china
                is not teeth
                        or rose.

But the sound we make
to try to keep from
words circling
                                        the room: yes.

The ocean of open doors: yes.
I am a swallow: yes.
Please keep it shut: yes.
                        Keep it

quiet: please.

You think   you know   about   this: no.

Each September, a little death: yes.

On the kitchen wall
the measured marks: yes   stopped
at 3 feet 5 inches
                like a frozen pond: yes.

Me: thin ice: yes.

You think we should try again?: no.
And never.
And I hate this conversation: yes.

Let quiet keep its rest: please.
A dying anything has too many hands: yes.

I have   cut off   each   finger:
                yes.
I have   burned down   the house

The door is always closed: yes.

I'm only a storm pipe
in someone else's
neighborhood: yes.

My smile a kicked-in flowerpot: yes.
        My mouth, this ugly shovel: yes.
I can never dig out: no.

And the whispers circulate: shhh.
        And the bus stop   moves.

Street corner eyes: make

                                        the front lawn a ghost

story.

The smallest thing missing: a tooth, a tombstone, a section of fence.

BEES WITH NO GOD

Lend me a God
to pray to tonight.

And I will pretend there is enough
earth left to kneel.

When it gets real bad the bees
in my stomach eat

until I'm no longer woman.
Just a hornet. A wall-less

plaything with picture-framed
stings. I lost the words

I put under
my pillow.

Watch how these breasts become a hive
without honey.

It's better for drones
to not know

their queen.
We extinct quietly

until we're almost winter.
A dying faith

of disappearing steeples
or dirty choir robes.

There's no one left
to sing.

SMALL THINGS

The webs of Walnut Creek are all spun
white. In our new town, I notice each
grocery store glare. Sticky stares
follow Omid down each aisle.

Still my love keeps quiet
hands. Wears kindness like salt
and pepper stubble. I study him
as he hums to houseplants.

It's been hard for me to learn a love
so gentle. To believe him when he chants
me close. Hushes *gorgeous* until I fall

asleep. In the morning, he scrambles eggs.
Spatula in hand, he spots the lonely
daddy-longlegs in a quiet corner. The wall weaver
nestled next to light. He says, *needing a home*
is such a small thing to be forgiven for.

He lets the delicate geometry
stay. I am slow to learn
how to handle a living thing. I study Omid

as he smiles at spiders. I ask him,
how? His speech soft as saffron, breath, a net
I lean against. He tells me he's been called a terrorist
more times than he can count. His answer: save something
smaller. Call each a guest. Leave all doors open.
Just because the world has called something
poison, he says, *doesn't mean we kill it.*

IV

Here's today. Jump. I promise it's not a lifeboat.

—OCEAN VUONG

BURN THE BOATS

Because I believed somehow
it was my fault: I never told
anyone how great grandmother pinched
the extra chub around my waist
and asked *who will keep you*
now? Pointed to every empty man
not at our table. Told me I'm only as good
as what I can please. Hunger

my only harbor. I carried this: a body
full of broken boards
and boundaries.
I never told anyone
how my first love dropped threats
like an anchor. Warned me
what would happen
if I took on water. Sinking always slipped
between his speech. I believed
being boarded equaled boat. So I floated
for seven years subtracting

what I had for another body. Parts
of me couldn't fit inside his hands.
My first love never let me use his front door.
Instead gave me a dark porthole
to climb through. I only remember this: in bed
he would measure the circumference of my thighs.
Then beg for less. I became the smallest vessel
I could steer. Every day he climbed through
my story. Until I gathered enough

distance to choose another
name. I can't turn back.
I strike a single match.
Burn myself   brighter.
The boats that built me
smoke on shore.

WHEN THE WAR COMES

you are black out/drunk at a party/he fucks you on a mattress/without sheets
you run/from hands wish for arms/when the war comes/you lose/your wine in a
bottle of names/when the war comes/you are only 16 have not learned/the word
combat/the war is here inside/this room/and you think/love is locking the door
you empty yourself/of mouth/crawl from him/a smudge of body/when the war
comes/you are unarmed in soupy dark/there is blood/on the mattress in this
room/passed through the hands of many/generals they never speak of bodies
they only blame the war

AT THE BAR MY FRIEND TALKED OF BODIES

About this skin she's forced
to carry. Meat for another.

She has met the butcher
and his growling

knife. Starves
what she can't

pronounce. I have whispered
in the dark

ever since I was old enough
to hollow.

No stomach can digest
shame: a congregation

of rocks. Patient in a
poisoned well.

We purge
or perish.

An empty mouth
unholied to the fast.

Our bodies drink away
their owners.

Hunger is never pretty.
Sadness sharpens the blade.

Most nights: a bottle of wine
steals my name.

And never gives
it back.

NAKED

He takes me in tiny bites
of bedroom. He is always there.
Feeds until I grow sick. My stomach
ripened.

He doesn't need a face.
Or name.

I give back garden
of blood, bone. The book
that named me. He licks his lips
as he watches. I don't believe in sin

or the many men. Liberty is sick
of being someone's woman.

Every night I take apart my breasts.
Clean my weapons. Cross them.

I sleep alone. Take my body.
But leave me words. Grieved
through grammar lust. Hollow

enough to fit inside a pretty
mouth.

I spelled my name with this war.
Carried this body. Targeted

and tender. Woman,
wear your blood
on the outside.

NO METAPHOR FOR MY MOUTH

not chainsaw
      or church.

                    I don't think of the things you did to me

as exit wounds
        or late night break-ins.

                  More like a play without scenery

a not-there forest
      a bird of unsong.

                        Do not clap for me.

Or this messy act
where no one pulls the curtain.

                                      Go.

I have no more lines memorized.

                    Nothing dainty

to make you

weep.

                Not oak
                    not Bambi heart
                        not bloodwolf teeth.

And yes, I know something

                  of the night

                     half eaten and thick.

It has

      it is

        it could be

                                          nothing

                                            maybe greed.

A cast of

unnameable trap

               doors that Venus fly

                    as soon as the house lights dim.

DEAR KEROSENE

I too have been bottled
and burned. At 13, I filled
duffle bags with empty
Marlboros packs and diet
pills, hid them behind floral
dresses in my closet.
When my mother found them
she did not tell me to stop.
I was raised arson.
Kerosene, their eyes
undressed you from oil.
Your body a body made
for other bodies. Lowercased
in the hands of many men.

I know you remember
their names. At 16, I let a boy
named Noah light my wick.
He finished fast. Never looked
at me again. Disaster is coming.
I hear you are the safest
bride. Made for Hurricane Lamp

or jet fuel. Men have stolen fire.
Tonight I wager her back.

I raze the house I live in.
I bluff then burn
each boat.
There is no retreat.

AND THE WOMEN SAID

watch as men call us lottery tickets.
Watch as they cash register us into gamble.
Into played out combinations of sweaty
bills and pocket want. Watch as they lick their lips
for that better life. Watch as they pout, when we don't
pay out. When the bling of our breasts doesn't make them
Cheshire Cat the same. We have our own debts
that need be paid: to mirrors, to mothers, to the way our hearts
traffic light in the closet after we sold ourselves

whole. And the women said feel the way we became campfire
how we ghost storied into this dangerous beauty. How those men
can't scrub out our smoke. Our blue learned to burn slow, standstill
like the moment between begging and maybe. Feel the way we soil
into shovel, how we let ourselves be held even after a matchbox tongue
misspoke of our flames. Even after we told flint, *you don't live here anymore*.
The women said feel how we are not open fields waiting for their strike.
They cannot not bury us deep, call us things of war and be surprised
when we landmine.

HOW TO STORM

Learn to rage. To rain so strong the oil of a lover rises to the asphalt. Become a cousin to freeway accidents and windshield wipers. Become a hurricane when you almost lose your mother. When she has more tubes than veins. When she wails naked in the hospital shower as you wash her. As you pray for one more night soaping her frightened chest.

Remember the first time you became a category five. Think how pressure drops at seven years old. Think of childhood baths. Of how your sister would never let you be the mermaid. Become a tornado of all the things you have spent. Hold up a pretty dress. Wild credit card receipts are blooming in the fields. Conjure a monsoon at your unpublished tender.

Listen to your downpour, like fists knocking on an empty schoolhouse. Like the rattling of windows in classrooms without heat. Scribble, scribble little earthquake, before your energy becomes someone else's I-knew-I'd-get-here. Don't let overcast kill you.

Go fist to fist with El Niño. Tell him, *I am the thing you didn't see coming.* Say, *just wait.* Next year, I swear, each and every newscaster will be calling my name. Oh yes. Say, *I can storm too.*[1]

---

1 *The last line is borrowed from the poem "As My Father Has His Heart Attack" by Jeremy Radin.*

NEW/PORT

Today I walk through
the town of me.
A fathered shoreline.
Eroded or chased.
The falling rain
of mother.
The ways to wreck
into gray.
Pieces of sisters
line the beach.
Boatbroken on shore.
Memory crackles.
The fire I build
in wine holds me
like a lung. Tight-
ened and tarred.
Shelled like a fist.
Call me oyster.
There is a part of me
worth keeping.

THE ONLY THING I OWN

Body, why can't I remember you
right? I know you're no life

boat. No sail-starved
wind. Your ode keeps

renaming. We become separate
seas. Come

closer. Don't worry. The doctors
opened your mother's heart

in time. Your father built his boat
inside a bottle. Body, I have wailed

amongst this squall
of salt. Have stung, sunk

and sung. Body, it's okay to be
afraid of each other.

To say *I don't know*
you before falling asleep.

Sorry I forget you.
Let's hold each other

honest as wind.

FOR OMID

I cut avocado open and wonder
at pit. How each half empties

and fills. Avocados summer inside
our home. I am braless and barely waking.

The house a still secret. Bed a museum
of our bodies bent and branched into hillside.

The way you squeezed my ripened
hips. Prefer me soft. A blur of morning stanza.

I run my fingers through dawn. Winter shivers
someplace else. I circle the recipe of your hands.

Rewind whispers. The tendertangle of ivory
curtains. Forest of your beard. You protect me.

Hours after I have left you
stuck behind a desk somewhere beige

hungry I open my lunch. The avocado
split in half. And I know somewhere

there is a tree that planted us.
A pit or concave, where we sleep

belly to belly.

LIFE/BOAT

Don't worry.
Your mother will always live
inside the house you built
for her. A sailboat can only wait
so long for wind. When you run
aground the buoys nod a quiet
I know. Omid loves you.
Anchor the children close.
At sunrise you write
about the morning after
your sister almost died.
Then your mother.
The many ways the sea tries
to take. They say *tell me*
a story and you never know
the right way to spill.
This is the one where you
and your father tied
yourselves to dark. Sailed
all night to make it
to Florida. Holding only a memory
of sleep. This was the biggest

goodbye. Your legs still
rock. Now in the mornings
you look at clouds you named
together. How each of you
chose your shape.

BOAT/BODY

There is not enough
distance between us

and the body. I beg
the women build

an ocean. Turn on tongue
and territory. Bargain

fire. Tease flames into family.
Taunt each island into telling

these stories still-birthed
in our bellies. A century

apologizes for someone else's
hands. I cradle my grandmother

ghosted into guilt. Can't forgive
this landscape. I will not kneel

for a man's affection. Women, keep
this world bloomdizzy.

Teach these teeth
to tender. We are swollen

with tomorrow. It's time to holy
one another instead. Salt water

saints. Crowned in sea foam.
The blue of each majesty.

They can't sink us
if we name ourselves
sea.

NOTES

Karen Blixen wrote under the pen name Isak Dinesen.

"Vesseled" is written after "Hydrophobia" by sam sax. It borrows the first line, "Here's how it happened."

"Mal de Débarquement" is written after the epilogue in *Voyage of the Sable Venus* by Robin Coste Lewis quoted in the epigraph.

"How the Body is Passed Down" is in conversation with an image from "Screens and Storms" by Natalie Shapero.

"We Know Monsters by Their Teeth" is in conversation from with "Planetarium" by Adrienne Rich.

"In an Attempt to Solve for X: Femininity as Word Problem" is written after Linette Reeman and torrin a. greathouse. It borrows structural inspiration from Reeman's poem "Childhood as an Unsolved Math Problem in an Infinite Number of Parts."

"How My Mother (Almost) Died" is written after "Dominique Dunne" by Amber Tamblyn. It borrows the structure of a timeline in reverse.

"Portrait of a Roofless House" is in conversation with "Sonnet LXV" by Pablo Neruda.

"The Surgeon General Named Loneliness a National Epidemic" is written after an article in the *Washington Post* titled "This former surgeon general says there's a 'loneliness epidemic' and work is partly to blame."

"Arson is a Family Name" is written in response to the white women who voted for Trump.

"I Want to Be Unclothed" borrows inspiration from "Diorama of Want" by Paige Lewis, particularly the phrase "wind still dangling from my teeth."

"Owned" is written after the poem "Sadness Workshop" by Stevie Edwards.

"What the Neighbors Saw" is written after "Dead Doe: I" by Brigit Pegeen Kelly.

"How to Storm" is written after Jeremy Radin and borrows his line "I can storm too" from his poem "As My Father Has His Heart Attack."

ACKNOWLEDGMENTS

Thank you to the following journals where these poems, sometimes under different titles and forms, have appeared.

American Literary Review—Life/Boat

Bayou—Burn the Boats

Best New Poets 2019—Small Things (reprint)

Chaparral—I Suggest Omid Shave His Beard, To the Lobster We Cooked at Kenyon

Cultural Weekly—How My Mother (Almost) Died, Daughter, Reasons I Haven't Done the Dishes, The Polite Bird of Story

Construction—Omid Tells Me You've Been Looking Less Puffy Lately, My Father Let Us Name the Boat: *Romance*, After, Arson Is a Family Name, Another Fight about Omid's Beard

decomP—I Am No White Dress

DIAGRAM—Lost at Sea

Diode—Boat/Body, Where No One Says Eating Disorder

Four Way Review—In an Attempt to Solve for X: Femininity as Word Problem

Glass: A Journal of Poetry—Closer

Hot Metal Bridge—Mal de Débarquement

Impakter—My Therapist Asks How the Dollhouse Was Built

Juked—When the War Comes, The Only Thing I Own

Muzzle—What the Neighbors Saw

Nashville Review—We Know Monsters by Their Teeth

PANK—There Is No Metaphor for My Mouth

Rattle—And the Women Said

Redivider—Hunger Is a Bride

Rise Up Review—Small Things

The Los Angeles Review—How the Body Is Passed Down

The Boiler—Storm Warning

The Penn Review—At the Bar My Friend Talked of Bodies

The Shallow Ends—Portrait of a Roofless House

Tinderbox—Owned

Sixth Finch—Bees With No God

SOFTBLOW—How to Storm, Dressing, Naked, I'll Never Return

Spry—The Boat of My Body

Up the Staircase Quarterly—My Father Tells Me Pelicans Blind Themselves, Dear Kerosene

Thank you to YesYes Books, to KMA Sullivan, Stevie Edwards, Jill Kolongowski, Devi Gonzales, Alban Fischer, and the rest of the YesYes crew. Eternal gratitude for believing in my work, and for your support, dedication and guidance. It is an absolute dream to be published by a press I so fiercely admire.

The biggest thank yous to sam sax, Paige Lewis, Jenn Givhan, and Tiana Clark who took the time and care to read and blurb this book, introducing *Boat Burned* to the world. I am forever grateful for your support and the way each of you has inspired and influenced my work.

Thank you Lara Zankoul for your photograph used as cover art. Thank you for your series The Unseen and your dive into the emotional depth through visual poetry.

My deepest gratitude to my amazing poetry family; you are my lighthouses, buoys and wind. You keep me floating. Without you I would have never had the courage to hit submit, or to show up to my first class. Thank you for sitting beside me as friends, mentors and family. Thank you: Julia Kolchinsky Dasbach, Tresha Faye Haefner, Victoria Lynne McCoy, Jason K. Watkins, Brendan Constatine, Kim Young, Alexis Rhone Fancher, Allie Marini, Brennan DeFrisco, Hollie Oveton, Heather Overton, Giselle Jones, torrin a. greathouse, Brian Sonia-Wallace, Jeremy Radin, Julia Campbell, Tanya Ko Hong, and more.

To the Get Lit-Words Ignite crew past and present. This calling, this love is what makes it all worth it. Thank you for helping me invest in the voice of tomorrow and to be a better teacher, leader, and poet for them, now and always. Thank you Monique Mitchell, Colleen Hamilton-Lecky, Mila Cuda, Raul Herrera, Hanna Harris, Marcus James, Austin Antoine, Veornika Shulman, Amanda Conlee, Sam Curtis, and Leslie Poliak.

A very special thank you to Get Lit's founder and Executive Director, Diane Luby Lane. You are a mother and mentor to us all. You changed everything for me, gave me a new world bursting with all this language and light. You are the reason I am here. The reason I believe the work is so much bigger than myself. Thank you for helping so many tell their stories. You ignite us all.

Deepest gratitude to my teachers, mentors, and friends who helped make this book possible and believed in my work. Your feedback has pushed me to have the most important conversations with myself and others, but most importantly the page. Thank you to (the one and only) Patricia Smith, Shira Erlichman, Stevie Edwards, Paige Lewis, Jericho Brown, Robert Pinsky, Carl Phillips, Matthew Zapruder, sam sax, Danez Smith, and Hanif Abdurraqib.

Thank you to the following institutions and organizations that supported the writing and editing of this collection through your fellowships and workshops: Tin House, Virginia Quarterly Review Conference, Kenyon Review Young Writers Workshop, Favorite Poem Project, The Poetry Barn, The Poetry Salon, The Writing Salon, In Surreal Life, and The Speakeasy Project.

To my incredible students at the Poetry Salon, Still We Rise, and Get Lit. It is an honor to learn from you all; thank you for helping me fall more and more in love with the work every time I have the privilege being in your presence.

To Poets4Progress: April Wells, Caitlyn Bove, Mila Cuda, Helen Drizhal, Kareli Flores, and more, thank you for your faith in me, and your commitment to always try to better. You made me a better mentor and human. You taught my heart so many important things. To Crystal Salas and David Hall for your feedback, community, and help in guiding these young voices and old souls. And for the circle at Kenyon.

To Mr. Murphy, my eleventh grade English teacher, thank you for always pushing me to do better, be better. Your challenging and encouragement changed my life forever.

To my dear dear friends who supported me, and loved me regardless of how they feel about poetry. Thank you for coming to readings and always cheering me on: Lauren Curnyn, Natalie Teichmann, Jackie Dondero, Christina Jahr, Tiffany Sprankle, Jess Tantum, Meg Minder, Krystin True.

To my in-laws, it is such an honor to join your family. Thank you for showering me with love and for your incredible son who is the best man I have ever met.

To my stepmom, Carol, who I dearly miss. Thank for you giving me my first writing job and always encouraging me through your passion and support. I always loved that you loved words as much as I did. Sending my love uptown.

To my aunt, Kathy, who is a fierce reader and tender-hearted cheerleader. Thank you for always supporting my poetry and artistic endeavors, even when they were nothing but poems about Diet Coke and teenage angst.

To my sister, Kat, who has always told me that creation is the holiest act. Thank you for teaching me about tenacity and spirituality, for showing me that whatever you can dream you can do and to never let anyone dull your sparkle. Love you lots.

Thank you to my parents for showing me that love means many things, but most of all it means standing by one another, no matter the seas. That what family looks like can change as frequently as wind, but it still fuels us, pushes us forward. That pain and love are not mutually exclusive, but a ship we all row together. Eternal gratitude for letting me share these stories, teaching me to sail, and introducing me to the mysticism and depth of the ocean. Special thank you to my mother, who taught me so much about giving and grace. Who has raised me to be both strong and a little more selfless. HATS.

And lastly, to my lobster, Omid. I never knew a love like ours could actually exist. Thank you for the emotional support, the permission, reminders and encouragement to write about it all. Time and time again, you remind me every story has impact, it is what connects us and helps us grow together. Thank you for pushing me to write about my stories as well as yours, in hopes they will reach out and take someone's hand. My life, even before we met, has always been one long love poem to you. I love you more than bacon.

And special thank you to you, the reader. Please know (cheesy as it sounds) I love you, even if I don't know you. I hope to one day read your words, or sit and talk about what has rocked you most. Thanks so much for reading. Sending you oceans of gratitude; without you none of this is possible. Shine on.

KELLY GRACE THOMAS is the winner of the 2017 Neil Postman Award for Metaphor from *Rattle* and a 2018 finalist for the Rita Dove Poetry Award. Her first full-length collection, *Boat Burned*, was released from YesYes Books in 2020. Kelly's poems have appeared or are forthcoming in: *Best New Poets 2019, Los Angeles Review, Redivider, Nashville Review, Muzzle, DIAGRAM*, and more. Kelly currently works to bring poetry to underserved youth as the Director of Education and Pedagogy for Get Lit-Words Ignite. Kelly is a three-time poetry slam championship coach and the co-author of *Words Ignite: Explore, Write, and Perform Classic and Spoken Word Poetry* (Literary Riot), currently taught in the Los Angeles Unified School District. Kelly has received fellowships from Tin House Winter Workshop, Martha's Vineyard Institute of Creative Writing and the Kenyon Review Young Writers Workshop. Kelly and her sister, Kat Thomas, won Best Feature Length Screenplay at the Portland Comedy Film Festival for their romantic comedy, *Magic Little Pills*. Kelly lives in the Bay Area with her husband, Omid, and is currently working on her debut novel, a YA thriller, titled *Only 10.001*.

ALSO FROM YESYES BOOKS

Stay by Tanya Olson

a falling knife has no handle by Emily O'Neill

Pelican by Emily O'Neill

The Youngest Butcher in Illinois by Robert Ostrom

A New Language for Falling Out of Love by Meghan Privitello

I'm So Fine: A List of Famous Men & What I Had On by Khadijah Queen

American Barricade by Danniel Schoonebeek

The Anatomist by Taryn Schwilling

If the Future Is a Fetish by Sarah Sgro

Gilt by Raena Shirali

Panic Attack, USA by Nate Slawson

[insert] boy by Danez Smith

Man vs Sky by Corey Zeller

The Bones of Us by J. Bradley

    [Art by Adam Scott Mazer]

CHAPBOOK COLLECTIONS

Vinyl 45s

    After by Fatimah Asghar

    Inside My Electric City by Caylin Capra-Thomas

    Dream with a Glass Chamber by Aricka Foreman

    Exit Pastoral by Aidan Forster

    Pepper Girl by Jonterri Gadson

    Of Darkness and Tumbling by Mónica Gomery

    Bad Star by Rebecca Hazelton

Makeshift Cathedral by Peter LaBerge

Still, the Shore by Keith Leonard

Please Don't Leave Me Scarlett Johansson by Thomas Patrick Levy

Juned by Jenn Marie Nunes

A History of Flamboyance by Justin Phillip Reed

Unmonstrous by John Allen Taylor

Preparing the Body by Norma Liliana Valdez

Giantess by Emily Vizzo

No by Ocean Vuong

This American Ghost by Michael Wasson

Blue Note Editions

Beastgirl & Other Origin Myths by Elizabeth Acevedo

Kissing Caskets by Mahogany L. Browne

One Above One Below: Positions & Lamentations by Gala Mukomolova

Companion Series

Inadequate Grave by Brandon Courtney

The Rest of the Body by Jay Deshpande